The Marriage Ring

A Selection of Three Sermons of
Dr. Martin Luther
on the Marriage Estate.

TRANSLATED BY
REV. J. SHEATSLEY, A. M.
PASTOR OF ST. MARK'S LUTHERAN CHURCH, DELAWARE, O.

THE BOOK TREE
San Diego, California

Originally published 1904
Lutheran Book Concern
Columbus, Ohio

New material, revisions and cover
©2003
The Book Tree
All rights reserved

ISBN 1-58509-014-X

Cover layout and design
Lee Berube

Printed on Acid-Free Paper
in the United States of America

Published by
The Book Tree
P O Box 16476
San Diego, CA 92176

FOREWARD

This book, *The Marriage Ring*, is the perfect wedding gift for many couples, having been written by the founder of the Protestant denomination of Christianity, Martin Luther. The three sermons he presents in this book reflect the immense value a couple should place on this holy bonding from God.

Ministers may also find these sermons useful because they, or portions of them, can be repeated and used in Protestant or Lutheran ceremonies. It would be a shame for us to otherwise lose or ignore the words of this important man—one of the most important in history. The book also contains the complete outline and wordings for a Lutheran Marriage Service, found near the back of the book.

This book is much needed today as statistics show that approximately half of all marriages will end in divorce. One will know from reading it exactly what is expected from a couple in marriage according to the Bible and in the eyes of God. Marriage is a very sacred union, and this small handbook will allow a deeper appreciation of what happens in marriage and what it really means.

The book was translated into English and first made available in 1904. It disappeared not long afterward. Reverend Sheatsley, the translator, expressed the same concerns about divorce at the time, but the situation today has only worsened. It is our hope that by sharing such words of wisdom, married couples will be able to make longer and more meaningful commitments.

Paul Tice

TABLE OF CONTENTS.

Luther and his family		Frontispiece.
Introduction	PAGE	5
Sermon on Heb. 13, 4	"	9
Sermon, based on John 2, 1–11	"	44
Sermon on Eph. 5, 22–33	"	85
Lutheran Marriage Service	"	112
Marriage Hymn	"	117

LUTHER AND HIS FAMILY.

TABLE OF CONTENTS.

Luther and his family	Frontispiece.	
Introduction	Page	5
Sermon on Heb. 13, 4	"	9
Sermon, based on John 2, 1–11	"	44
Sermon on Eph. 5, 22–33	"	85
Lutheran Marriage Service	"	112
Marriage Hymn	"	117

LUTHER AND HIS FAMILY.

INTRODUCTION.

WE do not intend to offer an apology for the publication of this little book. It needs none, at least not so far as its subject matter is concerned. Neither does it need an apology so far as the propriety of issuing these sermons in English, at the present time, is concerned. Look over the court records of the past few years and note the appalling number of divorces that have been granted in your county or state, or in the country at large. Observe too, as you have opportunity, how many homes there are that have been blasted as by an east wind, because marriage was either at the first an unfortunate one, or was afterwards abused and dishonored, but where the stress of unhappiness has not yet driven the person concerned to divorce as the final resort for relief. The condition revealed by our official divorce records should drive both the married and those who contemplate marriage to a most prayerful study of the institution of marriage, in order that they may the more faithfully and the more cheerfully meet its sacred obligations. The more so, since the basis of society is the home, and the basis of a happy home is marriage properly entered into and sacredly observed and honored in all its relations. To make happy marriages and thus to make happy homes and happy people is the object of these pages.

Luther wrote much more on the subject of marriage than the three sermons here translated, but a large amount of food poorly digested is less nourishing than a smaller amount whose properties have all been well assimilated. These three sermons, we believe, cover the field quite well, at least, as to essentials, and that is what we are aiming at. The first sermon is a full but simple explanation of the marriage relation. The second looks more at the practical aspects of the institution. The third is a matchless setting of marriage in the realm of the spiritual.

Of the three sermons taken together, the most striking characteristic is probably this, as it is of all of Luther's writings, that the facts, the relations and the duties of marriage are made to reflect upon the reader's mind solely in the full light of God's word. Luther pictures Christian marriage with the halo of heaven about it. There is a world-wide difference between his treatment of the subject and much of what is modern. This latter is done largely on the basis of mere ethics, or of rationalism, or even of materialism. Hence, too, much of the present day disdiscussion of marriage is insipid, nerveless and ineffective, not reaching the seat of the trouble. Some will, of course, be ready to criticise Luther with reference to some of his statements, most probably when he speaks of the relation of wife to husband. But all we ask of such critics is that they first be sure that they understand Luther. It would help them greatly to understand Luther on this point, if they would make a study of his home life — how he treated his own "Dear Katie."

The sermons were translated direct from the German, as given in the well-known *"Erlanger Edition."* The aim was to give a faithful translation, and at the same time to put it in readable English. How well this has been done, especially the latter, we do not undertake to say.

In regard to the divisions of the sermons into parts it may be said yet that in the case of the first Luther himself had indicated the parts. But in the second and third no such divisions are even hinted at in the original. For the convenience of the reader however and for the better understanding of the line of thought we tried to find and name the different parts. This was not easy to do, nor are the divisions made altogether satisfactory. Yet whatever fault may attach to them we believe this arrangement of the matter is to be preferred to having the entire discourse run on to the end without seeming stop or change.

Our prayer is that these sermons may go forth in this their new dress and in this their new Fatherland, doing much for the purification and elevation of the holy marriage estate.

THE TRANSLATOR.

MARRIAGE SERMON.

Heb. 13, 4.

(First published in 1536 A. D.)

THOUGH I have formerly often spoken and written about the marriage estate and life, yet, in honor of marriage, I will now also speak somewhat concerning it; for it is indeed one of the most necessary things in Christendom to preach about, and all Christians should have a knowledge of it. It is also the most common but at the same time the most prominent estate, by means of which all other estates exist and are sustained. For that reason, too, the apostles diligently write and admonish concerning it in their letters. We shall accordingly take up for consideration the short passage written in the Epistle to the Hebrews in the thirteenth chapter:

> "Marriage is honorable in all, and the bed undefiled: but whoremongers and adulterers God will judge."

Here the apostle does not, like a philosopher, teach heathen, but he teaches baptized Christians how to look upon and esteem marriage. They must not deem it unimportant, nor deal with it in a trifling and disgraceful manner, as the heathen have done and as the blind world always does, and as has hitherto been done in Christendom, where all praise was forcibly bestowed upon virginity, and matrimony in comparison was rendered altogether worthless. Just as though in that way all the world could be brought to chastity, when in fact everything is thereby filled with disgraceful whoredom. But Christians are to learn to honor and prize it as a Christian blessed estate, and are so to live therein that no harlotry or knavery may be found among them; which two things the apostle calls holding marriage honorable, and the bed undefiled. We will therefore see what the intent and force of these words are.

GOD'S WORD IS CONNECTED WITH MARRIAGE.

The first thing that one should learn concerning this estate, as also concerning all other estates, is this: each one should know and be convinced that matrimony has been ordained and established by God. This is about the most difficult thing in married life, namely, that one should learn to look upon this estate according to its highest honor, that it is God's institution and rests upon God's word. Nevertheless this view of matrimony appears to be a trifling matter, and every one imagines that he can do these things without the aid of a master. For who does not know that God established matrimony in Paradise and also confirmed it outside of Paradise, as Moses declares in Gen. chs. 1, 2 and 9? I also have often read these words and have learned to repeat them, but it is an art in which I am still not skilled, nor need I be ashamed, though I am an old doctor, to learn more about it daily. It is indeed not difficult to learn the words that marriage is an estate established by God, etc., but the difficulty to which I refer is this, that one be sure about this and feel no doubt, and that one look upon his own marriage and that of others everywhere as effected, ordered, sent and, as we say, provided by God. For the mad world, and indeed also prudent reason, do not take the matter seriously, but think it a matter of chance or an accident that one should get this or that person, just as when two persons, irrespective of marriage happen together.

Thence it is that marriage has come to be looked upon as a piece of jugglery and that it is so frivolously spoken of everywhere. The reason is that the world considers and judges the estate only according to the outward nature and appearance. For when the matter is taken under observation, the two, marriage and fornication, are very much related and the one seems so much like the other that, so far as cohabitation is concerned, there is no difference. It is therefore not such an easy matter to distinguish between the marriage relation and fornication, so that a husband may be quite sure in his mind and able to say, God has given me this woman that I should live with her; and likewise that a wife may say, God has given me this man, and with him I am to live by bed, table, etc.

I should like to see this above all things strongly impressed upon the minds of people, in order that for their sakes marriage may be honored and esteemed as good as possible. For it has been thoroughly corrupted by the unspiritual monks and sophists of the pope, who look at it only from without, according to its outward nature and works, and regard it as differing in nothing from an unchaste life; especially because they themselves are accustomed to such a life, yea, were utterly deluged therein, so that they were unable to think or say anything decent about it. And in addition the most holy among them have burdened the consciences of married people as with bands and ropes, directing what they must do with reference to the marriage obligation.

A Christian, however, should know how to make a clear and wide distinction between a married and an unmarried life. By what means? By means of God's word. For God has joined His word to the marriage relation by declaring in Gen. 1, 27. 29, God created them male and female, and gave Eve to Adam, blessed them and said, "Be fruitful, and multiply," etc., which blessing is renewed afterwards in the 9th ch. Likewise He says in ch. 2, 18. 24: "It is not good that man should be alone: I will make a helpmeet for him." "Therefore shall a man leave his father and his mother, and shall cleave unto his wife; and they shall be one flesh." Again in Matt. 19, 6: "What God has joined together, let no man put asunder." This is the jewel that seals the marriage estate with the honor of a divine work and institution. Without this word married life would be an unchaste life and no marriage. To be able therefore to see God's word in it is the most important thing in the marriage relation.

We may take for an example a similar case. If I should see a robber or murderer chop a man's head off, the deed would appear the same as when a ruler or judge orders a man's neck to be severed. Therefore, too, have they here persuaded the people with their preaching that this is a dangerous business, and have made the thing so horrible that men could not exercise this office with a good conscience. Thereby the civil sword has become dull and rusty, and men have been frightened from executing criminals. I myself have seen and known many fine, honorable men, who, when they were to sit in judgment upon some one guilty of a capital crime, fled elsewhere, in order that they might by all means not be present, nor be partakers in the horrible deed.

This and other errors all have their source in this that we look at stations and works only as they appear

Marriage Sermon.

in themselves and not in the light of God's word. For a murderer, when he chops a head off, does not do right therein, for he has no command nor word of God; yea, he does it contrary to God's word and command which says, Thou shalt not kill. Hence his murder is sheer darkness, hell and death. But when a ruler or executioner puts some one to death, then it takes place at the word and command of God. Then you do not wield the sword, but God Himself. Then the sword, through the word which commands the evil to be punished and the good to be protected and defended, shines as in the hand of an angel, yea, as in God's own hand. And just as a robber who commits murder is guilty of sin, since there was no command for it, so does a judge sin if he does not kill, for he has been commanded to put to death (Rom. 13, 4).

Likewise, if a thief should break into another man's house and should steal his clothing or other goods, it would appear very much like the act of a constable or other city official, who imposes a penalty upon a citizen or demands a pledge from him, yet there is a great difference between the two. The official acts in all justice as one who is authorized to take the pledge, and he exercises a holy and divine function. For God's word says to him, Wrongdoing thou shalt punish, righteousness thou shalt encourage and maintain. But a thief has neither right nor command to take what belongs to another; yea, God's word has forbidden him, which declares, Thou shalt not steal. Therefore are the hands with which he takes altogether devilish and cursed.

So also if two persons, a man and a woman, should live together in fornication, it would appear very much like married life. For they would clothe one another, associate and work together, be bed and table companions, just like married people, so that one with his reason could not distinguish between the two. But in married life God is present with His word, blesses and sanctifies the same and says, when you live with your wife as her bed and table companion, that is not a life as when harlots and knaves come together, but a holy and divine companionship, which God Himself has so ordered and ordained; just as a life of whoredom is forbidden, both here in this

Marriage Sermon.

epistle, and in the ten commandments, Thou shalt not commit adultery, nor covet thy neighbor's wife.

Therefore I say that it is Christian so to speak concerning matrimony and to praise that which is greatest in it, namely, that God has fixed His word upon it and has written it upon every spouse, so that every one should look upon his or her spouse as the only one and as though there were not another upon the earth; and that no king in all his adornment, yea, not even the sun, should in his eyes shine and glow more beautifully. For here you have the word by means of which God assigns and grants unto you this man or this woman, and says, This person shall be your husband, this person shall be your wife; thus I am well pleased and all angels and creatures are glad over it.

Oh, would to God that every one might have this feeling and be able to say from his heart, I am sure that God is well pleased that I should abide and live with my spouse, for He Himself has so established and ordered it and by His word has commanded me so to do. For this word comforts married people and secures a good conscience. But those who live together in fornication cannot enjoy a good conscience, since they have no such word of God; yea, they do contrary to that word and are not together in God's name, but in the devil's.

This would be the true golden practice in which few succeed well and which I myself cannot follow yet as I would. For we are ever yet hampered by the old habit of fixing our eye only upon the outward act and not looking at the matter according to the word. It is true that our flesh is full of wicked lusts which entice us to sin, but we must not follow them, nor judge this estate accordingly. On the contrary, if you take up God's word, by means of which this estate is blessed and honored, that will fully sustain you and ever comfort you anew, and it will render marriage a holy and spiritual estate for you. For it is doing the estate violence and injustice that it has been called a worldly estate. Other states, however, as of the pope, of monks and nuns, had to be called spiritual, probably for the reason that the devil, their god and founder who has invented and made them, is himself a spirit. For where in the Scriptures is there a word or a letter to the effect that a monk should wear a black or white cap, should belong to such or such an order, should eat this or that, etc.

But concerning marriage it is stated in the very beginning of Scriptures that God created them male and female, and gave them to each other, commanded them to be fruitful, to beget children, etc. Since now this estate has the word, yea, is contained in that word as in a case, so that in and through it the estate is made holy, it is but just that we hold it in great honor, and esteem it as a divine arrangement. Thus, then, may every husband and wife feel sure and certain that they are living in a truly spiritual estate which is pleasing to God, for they are not without but within the marriage relation, according to God's word, blessing and arrangement.

HOW TO RESIST TEMPTATION IN MARRIAGE.

Furthermore, this sermon is necessary not only for the sake of conscience, in order that you may have no scruples when you associate in a marital manner with your husband or wife, for God has so made and ordered it and is therewith pleased; but it also serves one against the devil. For those who have not yet entered into the marriage relation, but look upon it only from without, take it to be simply a life of pleasure and of carnal gratification. Such people, however, have never tasted nor experienced what God's word is, nor the power of God's blessing. In accordance with their lewd thoughts they only seek to gratify their lust in marriage and to have a good time. But afterwards, when they once have become married and find things otherwise than they expected, they know not how to adapt themselves to their conditions, for they neither consider nor see the word of God connected therewith. But if you regard the estate properly, how God's Word casts a halo about your wife's veil or your husband's head, then of a certainty the devil will approach you on every side and deluge you with temptations. First, he will create displeasure and disgust, in order that you and your spouse may not live together long in happy agreement, and so your pleasure and delight will doubtless soon give way to dislike. For he cannot endure the sight of married people living together in friendliness and unity.

Therefore, too, God permits that burning for one

another between the bride and groom, and says, "I must put a cap on the fool." For if this did not exist people could never be induced to marry. So much does the devil hate the estate; as he also otherwise, wherever he can, constantly opposes and interrupts God's word and work, and often succeeds in making man and wife sullen and afterwards impatient and bitter toward each other, so that their pleasure is turned into displeasure and their joy into anger and pain. Such is the daily experience of those who have not the needed grace to consider and believe God's word.

Therefore we read in Sirach, 25, 1. 2, that there are three things which are admirable and with which God and men are well pleased, namely, where there is concord among brethren, where neighbors love each other, and where a man and his wife get along well together. Why are these things praised so highly? Therefore, because it is a rare bird to find brethren living together in peace and enjoying a common pssession; or to see neighbors dwell together in a friendly manner, so that one may trust the other and expect the most of him; or to find married people living with each other in love and concord. When one observes these things only from without he may think: Indeed; is it such a difficult thing to be friendly toward your neighbor, to love your spouse, and that brethren should be united? If brethren are not united, who should be? Yes, but it is readily seen how these things go, when there is a little inheritance to be divided, how easily one takes the advantage of another and becomes his mortal enemy rather than to yield in the least. So, too, among sisters wrangling and brawls often arise over a bite of bread or a drink of water. The same thing often occurs between neighbors where nothing but faithlessness and malice appear, perhaps only because one chased the other's hen away, or some such thing.

So, too, man and wife may get to be at variance with no one more easily than with each other. By a single word, casually or jestingly uttered, one may so displease the other as to pierce his very heart, so that it can never be forgotten, and that afterwards, on this account, mutual poison and gall fill their hearts. The reason is this that the devil finds no pleasure in the existence of peace, concord and the like. If now they do not live in harmony, how can there be joy there or any other good thing? Therefore one should be prepared for the devil who is an enemy of this estate and who begrudges any peace and unity therein. One should be able to resist him with God's word and beat him back, and should always declare to the contrary. Be it as it may in regard to the devil's temptation, nevertheless this is a divine estate and God has placed me therein. If things do not always go as they should, patience is necessary. I should not and will therefore not reject the estate, nor despise it; for the estate is not bad, even if things do not always move along therein in the right manner. It is not always possible to have things so pure as though doves had made the selection.

Therefore, too, we say of married people who live together agreeably that their marriage is a happy marriage. As one may say, Here there is singular grace, and rarely does it succeed so well.

But it should occasion no surprise, if a married couple perchance do not love each other. For they do not see nor consider how their estate is contained and comprehended in God's word. For if they could see how they are surrounded by so bright a light and by sunlit rays, they would not become angry quickly, even if the cake were not all sugar; but they would consider that God has thus blended matters and has added a sauce to the roast, in order that God's word might taste the better. Therefore though anger and antagonism should arise, they can the more easily quiet and dismiss them with the thought, Here is God's word with which He has adorned and blessed this estate. This should be dearer to me than that I, through displeasure or otherwise, should corrupt this treasure and permit my spouse to be misled, whom God has given me.

Such is one of the ways in which the devil seeks to stir up all manner of dislike and variance in marriage, so that one gets to be as angry as a spider at the other. In this way wedlock becomes a very hell and work of the devil who laughs in his fist over his success. For do not think by any means that the devil and the world find joy and pleasure where love and concord rule. God and the Holy Spirit, however, are well pleased; He laughs and is happy over it. Therefore St. Paul and St. Peter admonish married people, if they should get to be at variance with one another, to get together again and become reconciled, so that their prayers may

Marriage Sermon. 25

not be hindered. For the beloved apostles well saw how the devil sows his seed among married people, so that even among Christians things rarely move along without anger and antipathy. Therefore the apostles want to comfort the people again with the word and restore peace.

But so matters are: An unmarried person thinks that if he were married, he would always laugh and be happy and would never say anything which might annoy the other. But in that you will quite probably not succeed. You think it something that can be done as a matter of course, the key to which is found in your own mind. No, marriage is called God's estate and order; therefore it must needs be harrassed by the devil, so that whoever enters upon the estate of matrimony enters an actual cloister full of temptation. Choose now whom you will, and however pious, rich, beautiful and friendly she may be, you shall find enough to do to preserve conjugal love and friendship. For to do this is not in your own power, and besides you have in your house a powerful enemy, called the devil, who from his heart is displeased at seeing things go as they ought. On the contrary, it would be pleasure and delightful music to him, if man and wife unceasingly growled and murmured at one another, and knocked chairs, benches and tables about the house. At such things he would laugh in his fist. For it is his desire, and as a disturber of divine works and arrangements he makes every possible effort to destroy altogether the estate of matrimony upon earth and to despoil it of every good fruit. Therefore you must not look at conjugal life with respect to the temptations and vexations of which it is full, but with respect to the word with which it is ordained and established. That word is able to convert your grief into gladness and your sadness into joy.

Then again, on the other hand, he will tempt you with indiscretion and unlawful desires. For, unless God has given you special grace, you will never be so chaste nor love your wife so truly, as not at times to think that some other woman is handsomer and lovelier than your own. Likewise your wife will never love you so much as not at times to imagine that some one else would please her better. Oh, God forbid! you say, shall I not love my wife? should I ever tire of my husband? Yes, God help me too! But con-

Marriage Sermon. 27

sider with me that, though you be chaste, yet in your heart you will experience just such thoughts suggested by the flesh or instilled by the devil. And especially will you find this to be the case, if you want to be a Christian.

Therefore you must arm yourself here also with God's word, which says: This is your flesh and your bone, given and adjoined unto of God. By means of this word your wife is adorned above all others upon earth, as it were with pure purple and gold and precious stones, so that you could not choose nor wish a better one. Thus you will be able to curb curiosity and to resist the devil, and not permit another to be more attractive in your eyes, nor please you better than your own, even though she should be repulsive, undesirable, queer and unfriendly to look at. But if you follow your own thoughts and the suggestions of the devil, which represent all other women as handsomer and lovelier than your own, then you have already spoiled the treasure and adornment in matrimony, together with its divine blessing and favor, and as a result there will be heard, on both sides, the lamentation that the devil must have directed me to this man or to that woman; may this or that thing happen to all who advised and helped me in this matter. If I had only married this or that person, for she is so very friendly and charming. Thus evil desires take a hand in the matter, as the poets say, so that love in the end rages and raves.

Therefore let every one see to it that he abide by the word, and that he view his spouse according to it, as bedecked of God with the finest adornment. If you keep that before your eyes, then your bed, your table, your chamber, your house and everything about your wife will become as it were pure gold in your eyes. For to this end you hear what God himself says to you, Thou shalt be the husband of this wife; and thou, wife, shalt keep thyself unto this thy husband; thus God has ordered it. If you look upon your marriage in this light and esteem it thus good and precious, then shall no other man's wife please you as well as your own. For the word will not permit it; even if you should imagine that another is of all, in words and demeanor, the most friendly and beautiful, yet in your eyes, compared with your own, she would be as black as coal and covered with the devil's filth.

Marriage Sermon.

For in her you do not find the ornament of God's word. But the prettiest and loveliest of all is your own wife, for her has God himself adorned for you with His own dear word.

But, as I have said, it is the most difficult thing to do to look upon this estate according to God's word, which alone renders both estate and persons lovely and removes all displeasure, anger, impatience and other temptations. And if some such thing should appear, it must disappear as if it had been swallowed up in the midst of the sea. For the word of God is something powerful and holy, and wherever it is known and embraced it makes all other things holy. But there is our failing; we are not always able to keep the word before our eyes, and often we allow ourselves to be surprised in forgetting it. And it were well, when we feel that we are tempted, to turn quickly again to the word before we found ourselves overpowered by the temptation. For we should not think that we shall not feel nor be subject to any temptation. For the devil will not desist; whenever he sees that we cling to God's word, he will seek all sorts of reasons, means and ways to snatch that word from our eyes and to move us to look and gaze elsewhere. If he succeeds in this, then he will soon also embitter the heart with aversion and impatience and fire it with inordinate lust, with the result that then every man or woman will appear prettier, more friendly and pious, or otherwise please you better, than your own spouse. Hence it is that one may see many fools who have the prettiest and most pious wives, but who nevertheless hang around shameful, nasty, filthy hags. It is all due to the fact that they do not have God's word, and do not view their estate different from an unchaste life.

In addition the flesh is also given to prying, and satiety is implanted in our very nature, so that we soon tire of those things which God has given us, even though we had everything upon earth. And this thing will not cease so long as we live, unless you hold fast to God's word. Thus the devil assists in the evil work, for he so blinds men that they do not see what an exquisite treasure they have in the word which portrays and appoints for each one a husband or wife, and in addition adorns them in the most precious manner, blesses and sanctifies them, in order that no one may look at another with a covetous or lustful eye. For whoever does this has already committed adultery, as Christ says in Matt. 5, 28.

This then is what the apostle wishes to teach here, when he admonishes Christians to view their estate of matrimony according to God's word, and therefore to hold it dear and precious and the bed pure and undefiled. For this, says he, is what God asks of you. But if you undertake to improve or change it, as the Pope with his beloved priests have done, then you shall not go unpunished. Pagans and Papists know nothing of this view of matrimony and hence have nothing fit to preach; yea, they deem it a carnal and worldly estate and have despised it and rendered it hateful, so that in comparison with the priesthood, falsely honored, marriage has been made repulsive, nor could any one find any pleasure or comfort in his conjugal life, notwithstanding that this above all things else should be impressed upon the conscience.

The apostle now, by declaring here that marriage is honorable and the bed undefiled, thereby places these two things over against the temptations that have been mentioned, viz.: that our flesh is full of hurtful lusts, and that both the desire for something different and the feeling of satiety are strong in us. The one drives me hither, the other thither, and lust impels me elsewhere. And this is not to be understood of keeping the bed and linen clean by washing, but this uncleanness and these spots in the marriage bed are, as he himself afterwards says, nothing else than fornication and adultery. For those who as whoremongers live an unchaste life outside of marriage, deem the estate as nothing, and despise and dishonor both God's word and the estate, no matter how pious they may pose before the world. The same is true of those who are in the marriage estate, who however do not keep it, but annul it contrary to God's command and order. In short, all those who look upon marriage as an estate that plumps by chance into one's lot, dishonor the same. For they do not see that married people are embraced in God's word, nor can they look upon a wife or a husband as clothed and adorned with that word. Therefore they do not hold it to be an honorable estate, but associate with it all manner of disgrace. For they are more pleased with a disgraceful lecherous life, than with that which is divine and or-

Marriage Sermon. 33

derly. Against this the apostle here warns them, that they should by all means take heed and so live that the marriage estate may be kept by them in excellence and honor as God's institution and order; namely, that they desist from a life of harlotry and enter the marriage estate. Afterwards, when they have once entered upon the same, they should take heed to themselves to keep the bed pure and undefiled; that is, that the wife should hold to the man and the man be content with his wife. If this is not done, then the beautiful adornment of God's word is befouled with the devil's filth and the bed defiled.

Therefore when the devil approaches you with the feeling of satiety and the lust for other things, see that you do the wise thing and seize God's word and say, God has created me a man and has placed me in this estate; this woman He has placed in my arms that she should be mine, etc. If you do this, you can the more easily keep your bed undefiled. For the word will fill you with fear and fright, yea, with nausea and horrors at others, and adorn your spouse so that, even though she should be repulsive, hateful, impatient, self-willed, she would still, for the sake of the word, be dear to you and please you better than another who might be decked with pure gold. For those, then, who can so regard and view marriage there is nothing more precious than the bridal veil, and no better adornment than the conjugal hat. That, then, is what we call properly honoring and praising matrimony and keeping the bed undefiled. For there is indeed no honor nor adornment, neither beauty nor any purity that stands higher than God's word.

MARRIAGE IS HOLY.

There are some wiselings who put forth reasons, showing why they need not marry, but who finally are completely drowned in fornication. These say that there exists nevertheless much wickedness in the estate of matrimony, and that through anger, impatience, evil lusts and the like, many sins are committed. No one indeed denies the fact that conditions here are not always pure and without sin as they should be. But on the other hand, show me anywhere a divine estate that is without sin. According to such a rule I would never dare preach a sermon, no man or maid would dare to be a servant, the government would never dare use the sword, nor any nobleman mount a horse. Not yet, my dear fellow; in our life here we shall never become so pure as to be able to do any good work without sin. The article: "I believe in the forgiveness of sins," must stand. And daily we need to say in the Lord's Prayer, "Forgive us our tresspasses."

Therefore I will hear of no exception in the case of this estate. Sin here, sin there; if you want to stick one estate into sin, then stick the others in also; if you want to draw one out, then draw the others out also. I have never preached a sermon, nor do I ever expect to preach one, that has been without sin. I shall continue to be a sinner, and I shall let the article concerning the forgivness of sins stand, and shall not deny it. If at times husband and wife get angry at one another, that is sin and a wrong; but over against that forgivness of sin will only be the greater, if they but continue within the proper sphere and do not step outside of it, but live on in the estate into which God has called them. For although the estate is not maintained without sin, yet God's word is so great that for its sake the estate itself is pure and holy.

If this is not so, I will say still more; if you want to look at the matter in that way, how we are all born in sin from Adam, then the whole estate of matrimony, even though it be well and properly maintained, is sinful and impure; just as in the case of heathen and unbelievers who do not have God's word, all their life and all their works are damnable in the sight of God.

Therefore it must be noted well here how the apostle speaks concerning matrimony, and declares from the mouth of God that, so long as adultery and fornication are avoided, the estate among Christians is to be held and esteemed honorable and pure. For if we should consider the fall of Eve and our nature, then the estate would not be honorable and pure in the sight of God. For otherwise carnal passion and other sinful desires would not have existed in Paradise, nor would one person have felt any shame in the presence of another; they would not have covered or clothed themselves, but man and wife would have associated together without any evil lust or passion, and as one picks an apple from a tree, so children would have been begotten and born without any labor

Marriage Sermon.

or pain. But now conditions are so that no man and woman can associate without feeling the movements of shameful passion. Wherefore we read in Psalm 51, 5, "Behold, I was born in iniquity, and in sin did my mother conceive me." And all the saints also, who lived in the estate of matrimony, had to confess that they were not exempt from these evil desires. And therefore, too, Christ did not want to be born in the natural manner from man and wife, but chose a virgin for His mother and sanctified her flesh and blood, to the end that His birth might be a pure and holy birth.

But the apostle now declares here that God wants to be gracious toward this estate, and, though it is indeed impure by nature, yet it shall not be impure among Christians and those who believe; but the marriage bed shall henceforth be called undefiled, not of itself, nor because of our nature, but because God covers it with His grace and does not impute natural sin or uncleanness, implanted in us by the devil. Go on then and purify the estate with God's word, in order that it may be a divine and holy estate; not thus, as though God should remove conjugal desire or love, or forbid marital deeds, even if these things do not take place without sin. For so the Pope teaches that this estate is impure, and that one cannot serve God and be married. But the apostle declares the estate to be pure for this reason, because God in His mercy declares it to be pure, and does not impute to it the sin inhering in our nature.

So God also said to Peter, Acts 10, 15: What I have cleansed, that call not thou common. That which otherwise was unclean and forbidden is here rendered clean and holy, simply through God's declaration. So also is the case of marriage. Since God purifies this estate with His word and calls it a chaste and holy estate, we also are to deem it holy. Yet one should know that this purity is not of nature, but is purely the fruit of grace which blots out and covers the natural uncleanness and sin. For just so, too, does He remit the whole of original sin in the case of those who are baptized and who believe that through the Savior Christ they secure the forgivness of sin and are made children of everlasting life. For although this original sin still clings to our flesh and is active so long as we are upon earth, yet we, who are Christians, are called pure and holy, because He overshadows us with the cross, and in addition sends the Holy Spirit who begins to purge away sin and who keeps on purging until death. Accordingly we are indeed not without sin, yet we have the verdict from heaven, spoken by the mouth of God, that we are now pure and holy; and this is so because the beautiful heaven of mercy, which is Christ with His purity, righteousness and holiness, is spread over us, covers and embraces us, and because we have been made members of His body through baptism and cling to Him by faith.

So also, I say, does He deal with the estate of matrimony. Though sin and evil lust are indeed associated therewith, from which the saints even are not exempt, yet He throws His mantle over married people, and declares them pure through His word. This is the beautiful covering cast over the bridal or marriage bed, and by means of this it is adorned and rendered beautiful, pure and undefiled. Therefore the apostle admonishes married people to consider the fact that God declares the estate pure and spreads this covering over it. And they should therefore also be thankfull and should see that the marriage bed, which God has purified, cleansed and adorned, is not by them rendered unclean again and bespotted with adultery and fornication.

MARRIAGE IS HONORABLE.

Furthermore, the apostle does not only want to have the marriage bed declared undefiled, but also requires that marriage itself be held honorable. Hereby sinful lust and other weaknesses are still more effectively covered, for not only is the estate declared pure, but also, through God's word and command, honorable and precious, concerning which more has already been said. This, then, is not simply to put the bride and groom to bed and to cover them, as one might say, but also to adorn them to the utmost and to conduct them to church in the most honorable manner.

For here He adorns them with that which is far more beautiful than any necklace of pearls or precious stones, namely, the fourth commandment: "Thou shalt honor thy father and thy mother," etc., for this also implies honoring the marriage estate. Likewise the sixth: "Thou shalt not commit adultery." With these words He commands you to live with your

Marriage Sermon.

spouse and be contented, and promises that if you do this, it shall not be called sin, but a blessed estate and well-pleasing to Him. Likewise in Gen. 2, 24, He so confirms and strengthens the marriage bond as through it to set aside even the righteousness and authority of parents, or at least to lessen these, when He says, "Therefore shall a man leave father and mother and shall cleave unto his wife." Again, soon after the fall He blesses them again, promises them the seed of the woman, and clothes and adorns them himeslf.

And with our own eyes we observe how God continues to honor this miserable flesh and blood that is born and lives in sin, since He is constantly blessing it and making it fruitful, so that all the saints come forth from the marriage estate and this whole life has its origin there. For that reason, too, the first mother received the name Eve, which means the living one, or mother of the living. And how could God commend the estate more highly than just by this that also in the New Testament He calls it undefiled and holy?

Therefore also we are to esteem this estate honorable and exalted, and are not to do as those who, like unclean swine, think and say nothing concerning it but what is in accord with their own shameful fornication and adultery. Shameful, nasty fellows are they, who befoul their own nests and who, like swine, take pleasure in rooting in filth with their unclean snouts, and in wallowing in their own shame. But Christians are to hold their estate honorable and decent, just as they see that God himself does; and if there should be some impurity associated with it, they are to cover and ornament it, just as God does not account that to be sin which by nature is sin, but throws a covering over it and makes it decent and honorable.

Likewise we should not do as those hostile wiselings who are ready to find fault with the estate and to reproach it, because there is much unpleasantness, contention, care and labor connected with it, and who say, May God defend me against this estate; whoever takes a wife gets a devil. These are the poisonous dogs that with their vile mouths slander the dear estate and mutilate it with their poisonous fangs, just as those swine defile it with their snouts. For the devil

Marriage Sermon. 43

always finds great pretense for speaking against the estate, since he sees both original sin in it and the sorrow, care and labor connected therewith. These two things he can use to good advantage and by means of them he seeks to mislead every one with respect to matrimony and to spoil the estate entirely in their eyes. Therefore we need the more to exalt and praise the estate, and the more to honor, adorn and beautify it, just as we hear how God himself does. Let the devil by means of his swine and dogs keep on abusing and reviling, and let them take their reward which their god the devil shall give them. But learn thou to look at the estate and to esteem it as God's own work, purified and made holy through the word of God. And whoever lives in this estate, let him comfort himself therewith, and let him thank God that he is so well-pleased with it as to spread a covering over it and in addition so gloriously and beautifully to adorn and praise it.

Let these things be said at this time to the honor of marriage and the marriage estate. May God give us grace that we may thus believe these things and so live in them. Amen.

SERMON ON MATRIMONY.

John 2, 1-11.

(Delivered in Wittenberg in 1525, first published in 1560.)

DEAR friends, since you have heard the Gospel, how the Lord Jesus Christ, Son of God and of the pure Virgin Mary, in company with His beloved mother and His disciples, went to the marriage at Cana of Galilee, I shall now say something concerning the estate of matrimony, for the comfort both of those who are married, but especially for those who think of entering upon this estate; and I have the confident hope that if we receive and retain these things in our hearts, they will not be without abundant fruit and usefulness both to body and soul. I shall therefore in this sermon, if time will permit, treat these four parts: First, I shall speak of the great honor of the marriage estate. Secondly, what those should do, both men and women, who expect to enter upon the estate of matrimony, how they should begin it in a godly manner. Thirdly, how persons who have married should live together as Christians. Fourthly, whether man and wife may also again separate. These are the four points which by the grace of God we shall consider to-day.

We will now listen to the first part.

THE HONOR OF THE MARRIAGE ESTATE.

We justly call it a holy order and estate which, as the Scriptures show, God has graced with eight kinds of honor. The first honor is this, that marriage was not instituted nor ordained by an angel or by men, but is a created work of God, consisting of man and wife. For thus we read in Gen. 1, 27, God created them male and female, and God blessed them and said unto them, Be fruitful and multiply. Now the Hebrew word for God here is in the plural, *Elohim,* the Gods, which indicates that thre is more than one person in the Godhead. The same word is used in verse 26, "Let us make man." This cannot refer to angels as the reprobate Jews falsely affirm, for the angels did not create any men. But this is said of the entire holy Trinity, as Father, Son and Holy Ghost. Matrimony is therefore the created work, order and institution of the entire holy Trinity. So, too, Moses writes, in the second chapter, that the *Elohim,* the Gods (not *Eloha* in the singular, God, one person alone, but) many persons in the Godhead, made Eve from one of Adam's ribs in his sleep. There we read according to the Hebrew, And the Gods brought her to the man, but in German, God brought Eve, the woman, to Adam; so that the entire holy Trinity acted as bridesman and conducted Eve to her spouse. Yes, that even the Son of God, Jesus Christ, as the true superior Highpriest, married and blessed Adam, the groom, and Eve, the bride. For the words which Adam uttered in Genesis 2, 24, were spoken by God Himself, as Christ in Matt. 19, 5, and Mark 10, 7, says. Of a truth this was Jesus Christ, who is true God, through whom God the Father spoke.

Now consider, dear friends and children, whether this is not a mark of great honor for the estate of matrimony, that it is a work of God, instituted by the entire holy Trinity who was the real bridesman,

Sermon on Matrimony.

and that Jesus Christ, the Son of God, married, consecrated and blessed Adam and Eve as man and wife.

If now an emperor, being a distinguished person, should ordain and institute something, how would men not boast concerning it and eulogize it as a high, imperial establishment? What now is the emperor, a mortal man, in comparison with God? Nothing else than a pound of lead compared with a great mountain of gold.

Here then we should boast in our hearts and highly esteem this ancient institution of the entire holy Trinity, and should thank God and pray Him that we may be found in it according to His holy will.

O, if the order or state of monks and nuns had such credit, that it was God's order and institution, how would they vaunt and brag? Indeed, the world could not endure their boasting, for we have seen already with what boldness they boast of Francis, Dominic and Benedict who instituted and established their order, but who were only men. But that matrimony is God's order and institution, that we esteem lightly. O, the blindness of men!

The second honor which belongs to the state of matrimony is this, that it was not instituted in Athens of Greece, nor in Babylon, nor in Rome, neither at Compostel of St. James, but in the holy Paradise, in the garden of Eden, which God himself planted and in which He placed the tree of life. If something would have ailed man, he could have eaten of this tree and he would have found relief.

How men esteem an institution which has been established at Compostel in Spain or at Rome, though it be but the work of a poor, miserable man. Much holier and higher is matrimony to be esteemed, which was instituted and established in holy Paradise which God, after Adam and Eve were driven out, guarded with a glittering fiery sword in the hand of an angel or cherubim, so that no man in the future could enter in (Gen. 3, 24).

The third honor is this, that the patriarchs, priests and prophets lived in the state of matrimony. Such were Adam, Enoch, Noah, Abraham, Isaac, Jacob, Joseph, Moses, Aaron, Eleazar, Isaiah, Hosea, Zechariah, Ezekiel, excepting Daniel, Elijah and Elisha who, I believe, did not have wives. Likewise Jeremiah

Sermon on Matrimony.

whom, as we read in chapter 16, 1. 2, it was forbidden in particular to take a wife. All the rest were married.

This now is again a great honor for married persons, that they can say: God be thanked and praised, I am not like monks and nuns, living in a new estate that did not exist a thousand years ago, but my estate existed more than five thousand years ago, and in it lived the patriarchs, priests and prophets. If God was so well pleased with those holy people, surely He will be well pleased also, if I with my beloved wife or husband live in this estate.

The fourth honor is this, that God has applied an earnest prohbition to the estate of matrimony. It is like a man who has a beautiful garden of aromatic flowers or roses. He admires it greatly and does not want any one to go in and pluck flowers or molest anything, and therefore he puts a hedge about it. Thus has God done with the sixth commandment: "Thou shalt not commit adultery." Since matrimony is His dearest flower garden in which the most beautiful roselets and pinks bloom, for these are the dear children which are created in the image of God and which are born in matrimony and come from it, in order that the human race may be preserved; therefore, God commands that matrimony be kept in the fear of God and in all propriety and honor and be not annulled.

For God will fearfully punish, in body and soul, him who violates this estate and will cast him out of His kingdom (1 Cor. 6, 10). This is shown, too, by the destruction of the whole world, excepting eight persons, by the flood (Gen. 7, 22.23). Likewise the overthrow through brimstone and fire of the cities of Sodom and Gomorrah (ch. 19, 24. 25). So also the manner in which God, because of his adultery, punished king David, His most beloved servant (2 Sam. 12, 10-12). Thus, furthtrmore, God punished the Gideonites who violated the wife of a certain Levite. For when the Benjamites would not punish the crime but even sought to defend it, 25,000 men of Benjamin, all men of war, were smitten down and slain (Judges 19, 25. 29 and 20, 46).

Surely adulterers, harlots and rulers who remain silent and wink at these crimes, should be filled with terror, if they are at all men, when they consider these fearful examples of God's wrath.

Marriage Sermon.

The fifth honor of matrimony is that which God commanded in the Old Testament, as we find written in Deut. 24, 5, "When a man hath taken a new wife, he shall not go out to war, neither shall he be charged with any business: but he shall be free at home one year, and shall cheer up his wife which he hath taken." This is surely something great that God for a year relieves and frees the young couple from war and all annoyance, in order that they may be happy together.

And here we learn, too, that God is well pleased when young married people live merrily together. Is this not a great honor and comfort for married people? Indeed, if it were written that God had freed monks and nuns, during the first year of their convent life, from all care for the common good, and that they should spend their time in singing; God forbid, what boasting and vaunting would there not have come from it? But since this is written of married people, nothing is said. And so it always is: what God has done is passed by in silence, but man's work is eulogized to the utmost.

The sixth honor is this that also our Lord Jesus Christ, the Son of God, was not born of a mere single virgin, but of Mary, who, as Matthew 1, 18 and Luke 1, 27 state, was betrothed to Joseph, her husband, as his lawful wife, as the angel declares. Likewise the law of Moses in Deut. 22, 23. 24 says of a virgin, betrothed to a man, but not yet known of him (even as Mary was not yet known of Joseph), that she is the man's wife. Accordingly our Lord Christ was according to the law, born in wedlock of Mary His mother, for she was betrothed to Joseph her husband, and He has thus honored that estate by His birth.

The seventh honor is this that our Lord Jesus Christ, at the age of thirty, after His baptism, when He is about to enter upon His public ministry, first attends a wedding among the peasants, at the village of Cana in Galilee, and honors matrimony as the work, order and institution of His Father, of himself and also of the Holy Ghost and hence of the Holy Trinity. He also takes with Him His mother and the disciples; the former assists in the work and the latter play the part of servants. Is this not a great honor, yea, much greater than if emperor, king and princes had been there.

O, if monks and nuns had some such reputation and

Marriage Sermon.

honor, that Christ was present when one became a monk or a nun, God forbid, how would this not have been proclaimed from every corner and pulpit? Yes, in addition, with red colors and gilt letters it would have been written in every book and painted in every church. But since it is written how Christ, the Son of God, in company with His mother and disciples, attended a wedding, it is considered a common thing or work.

The eighth honor is this that our Lord Jesus Christ does not stop with simply attending the wedding (which consisted of but three tables of guests, as the word *architriclinus* indicates), but there for the first time, as St. John tells us, manifests forth His glory, that He is the true, almighty, eternal God and God's Son, and made red wine of the white, clear, transparent water with which the servants had filled the six stone water pots. For so the church sings in the hymn, *In Die Trium Regum: "Aquae rubescent hydriae."* (The water pots blushed and grew red.) And in the holy promised land the wine usually grows red, red as blood, for which reason, too, the Holy Scriptures call the red wine blood (Gen. 49, 11. 12).

Furthermore, Christ does not give them an ordinary common present, but a worthy one. For, as St. John writes, each of the stone water pots contained two or three firkins. Now a firkin is equal to about nine gallons, so that each pot was large enough to contain about twenty gallons. There were thus about one hundred and twenty gallons of wine that Christ gratuitously made for the wedding feast. Besides, it evidently was not of an inferior quality, but the best, as appears from what the governor of the feast said to the bridegroom, "Every man at the beginning doth set forth good wine; and when men have well drunk, then that which is worse; but thou hast kept the good wine until now."

Surely it is a great honor and comfort to married people to hear how Christ, though He be the Son of God, cares for them nevertheless, will be with them at the wedding, that is, in the state of matrimony, will not suffer them to want for things to eat and to drink, nor let them come to shame, but will provide them with what they need for their fill; and rather than have them suffer, He will make wine out of water, that is, turn their sorrows into joy and cheer, and will in no way forsake them, as we read in Ps. 34, 10: "The young lions do lack, and suffer hunger: but they that seek the Lord shall not want any good thing." Likewise in Ps. 37, 25: "I have been young, and now am old; yet have I not seen the righteous forsaken, nor his seed begging bread."

It may be added here, too, that some of the church fathers, as Bonaventura, maintained that the groom and bride at the wedding in Cana were John the evangelist and Mary Magdalene, as would appear from the sequence on St. John's day. However, I do not hold to this view, but rather believe, as the old Greek teacher, Nicephorus, who lived at Constantinople four hundred years ago, during the reign of the Grecian emperor Emanuel, writes, that it was Simon the Canaanite, a son of James by a sister of the mother of our Lord Jesus Christ.

And it is quite reasonable and credible that the bridegroom and the bride must have been closely connected with the holy mother Mary and been her near relatives, because she herself was there and helped to oversee matters and took care that there was something to drink, when the wine was all.

For the dear mother Mary would not so readily have mixed in among strange or distant relatives at a wedding or feast, since other near relatives would naturally have been present. Wherefore they also as poor wretched peasants, together with their nearest friends, joined themselves to Christ and held to Him, in human fashion, as poor simple friends are accustomed to do (Matt. 13, 55).

And again, according to Matt. 11, 19 and John 6, 42, the Lord Christ appears in the capacity of a man (Phil. 2, 7) and sustains a friendly and brotherly relation to them. Not a glance of His divine majesty appears here, but the extremest form of a servant. Shame on thee, thou poor human prudence or reason, that thou dost not think of this, nor consider it.

These now, beloved friends, are the eight things with which, as ye have heard, matrimony is honored. We now proceed to the second part.

HOW ONE SHOULD ENTER UPON THE MARRIAGE ESTATE.

Three things are necessary in order to enter upon matrimony in a godly and Christian manner. The

Sermon on Matrimony.

first, that one begin in faith. The second, that one in prayer ask God for a pious partner. The third, that one take the step with the knowledge and consent of parents.

In the first place, to begin in faith means that one should first consider God's word as we read in Gen. 1, 27. 28: "Male and female created He them. And God blessed them, and God said unto them, Be fruitful and multiply." Likewise ch. 2, 18: "It is not good that the man should be alone: I will make him an help meet for him." This is the sure word of God which does not lie, and on the strength of it one should marry and should believe firmly that matrimony, in its very nature and with all its works, sufferings and whatever belongs to it, is a thing pleasing to God Himself. Then a person can say in his heart, See, dear Lord God, I learn here that matrimony is Thine own work and is pleasing to Thee. Upon Thy word therefore will I enter upon it, and however Thou wilt deal with me in this relation, I will be satisfied and pleased.

Whoever marries on the strength of this word of God and understands that matrimony is God's creation and work and is pleasing to Him, will find joy and gladness in it, though another, who does not know nor consider God's word, will experience nothing but displeasure and misery.

And here is realized the truth of what we read in Prov. 18, 22: "Whoso findeth a wife findeth a good thing, and obtaineth favor of the Lord." And to find a wife means, through God's word, to be sure in one's heart that God is pleased and delighted with his estate, work and condition in life (Ps. 128).

For that reason many have wives, but few find wives. Why? They are blind and cannot observe that it is God's work and pleasing to Him that they should live and be occupied with a wife. If they should discover this, they would find heartfelt pleasure in any wife, no matter how repulsive, cross, mischievous, poor or sick she might be; for they could always hold up before God His own work, creature and will. And since they see that it is God's good pleasure, they, like the martyrs, would experience peace in suffering, pleasure in displeasure and joyfoulness in the midst of tribulations.

But here lies all the trouble; we judge God's work according to our feeling and do not consider His will,

Sermon on Matrimony.

but only our wish. For that reason we do not understand His work and are compelled to make evil of what is good and to find displeasure where there is pleasure. Nothing is so evil, not even death itself, but that it will become sweet and tolerable, if I only know and am certain that it is pleasing to God. Forthwith there follows what Solomon saith, He shall obtain favor from the Lord.

This then is what it means to begin in faith; that one look to God's word and be certain that this state is pleasing to God, and that one will therefore not allow cold nor heat, trouble nor labor to grieve him.

The second thing is this, that one earnestly petition God and call upon Him for a pious spouse. For thus says Solomon in Prov. 19, 14, "House and riches are the inheritance of fathers: and a prudent wife is from the Lord." And Christ says, Matt. 19, 6, "What therefore God hath joined together, let no man put asunder." We see clearly here that a pious spouse is from the Lord and is a gift of God; just as Adam, our first ancestor, did not find a wife himself, for God alone gave him Eve. Since then a pious spouse is a gift of God, you should first of all, before you undertake anything else, ask God (James 1, 5, 6,) that He may give and provide you with a pious wife or a pious husband.

God indeed could do this without your prayer, but He does not want to. It is His will that you should first honor Him and know that it is His gift, that you should earnestly petition and call upon Him and say in your heart, Ah, dear Lord God and Father of our Lord Jesus Christ, provide and give me, Thy poor child, a pious husband, or a pious wife, with whom, by the grace of the Holy Spirit, I may live in the state of wedlock in a godly manner.

But some there are who are so prudent that they might well say, Why, God forbid, should I pray for a man or a wife? That would be a shame. Others there are who, if you teach these things from the pulpit, will laugh and scoff at them. But, dear son and daughter, you need not consider it a disgrace to pray for a pious spouse, for you surely do not consider it a disgrace to ask God to grant you a healthy hand or limb.

Now, a pious spouse is just as needful as a sound hand or limb. For if your husband or wife proves uncongenial, you will enjoy few happy days or hours, and instead thereof you would rather suffer with a lame hand or leg. Nor dare you look at it as a thing to laugh and scoff at, for if marriage is to be a success, it must be begun with God. Do not therefore be ashamed to call upon God. But if you begin of yourself without prayer, then, if it proves a failure, you dare not blame God, as Eve and Adam did after the fall in Paradise, but blame yourself. Also laugh and scoff at yourself; why did you not ask God for a pious or good spouse?

Therefore parents also, before they consent to their children's marriage, should themselves go to church and pray in their hearts and say, O almighty God and Father of our Lord Jesus Christ, Thou who hast given me a son or a daughter, provide and give them a good Christian spouse and by Thy Holy Spirit help them to live a godly married life, for the matter rests with Thee alone, and with no one else.

Thus we read concerning Abraham (Gen. 24, 2 sqq.) that he prayed, when he commanded his servant who was steward over all his goods, to go to the city of Nahor in Mesopotamia and get a wife for his son

Isaac. And when the servant said, How if the woman will not follow me unto this land; must I bring thy son again unto the land from whence thou camest? And Abraham said unto him, Beware thou of that. The Lord God of heaven, which took me from my father's house, and that sware unto me to give this land unto my seed, He shall send His angel before thee, and thou shalt take a wife unto my son from thence.

It is as if he should say, If God means to give my son this land, then He will also give him a wife, for I have called upon Him and prayed for it. Therefore I will also command Him to do so. Thus he boldly trusts and relies upon God's promise and upon prayer. But if God will not grant it, then come again, says he. He surely knows what needs to be done. Yes, he adds yet, He will send His angel before thee. So surely does he comfort himself in his God and with His promise. And the matter was accomplished, too; and Isaac, Abraham's son, secured the beloved Rebecca, a very pious, God-fearing child, as his wife. And if we do with our children as Abraham did, we will find that the result will be just as favorable as it was in his case. If we do not, then we may take heed and watch, for it will go ill with us and crying and lamentation will follow. This, then, is the second thing, viz., that one should pray and call upon God for a God-fearing spouse.

The third thing is this that one marry with the knowledge and consent of parents and do not betroth oneself secrectly in a corner. For there is the fourth commandment of God, "Thou shalt honor thy father and thy mother" (Ex. 20, 12). For so long as children have not been given in marriage by their parents, they are under the power of father and mother, and these should exercise authority over them. For there is no greater obedience than obedience to father and mother, neither any greater authority.

No son or daughter therefore should enter into a betrothal secretly without the knowledge and will of the parents; for it is a great sin against God's fourth commandment, which commands children to honor their parents.

For children who betroth themselves secretly not only do wrong, but also do a foolish thing, since marriage, if it should prove unhappy, is a dangerous step and will be tedious and full of trouble. For throughout their entire life they must be plagued and must put up with misfortune, and no one but death can come to their relief. And it is to be feared, if one despises father and mother and marries without their knowledge and consent and thus begins matrimony in sin, that God will add neither success nor happiness.

But if children kept God's command, obeyed father and mother, God would then love them and add His blessing and every other good thing to their married state. Experience also teaches that children, who betroth themselves secretly without the knowledge of their parents, are rarely happy in their marriage; contention and strife usually exist and their life is full of misfortune. For they began in opposition to God and His command and therefore there can be no happy issue. Therefore, too, it would be better if parents accustomed their children not to be ashamed to ask them for a partner. Parents should observe, too, that they should advise their children, in order that these may the more readily and hopefully restrain themselves and wait.

Accordingly it would be proper for a child to say

Sermon on Matrimony. 65

to father and mother, Dear father and mother, with your consent I should like to get married and choose such or such a person. Yet I shall leave it all to you; whatever you say, I shall be satisfied.

But it is considered a great disgrace that one should ask his parents for a spouse. Yet one is not ashamed to ask parents for a coat, cloak, house or something else. For that reason, do not be ashamed to ask of your parents a spouse, who is far more important and necessary for you than a coat, cloak or house. These things, if you are not pleased with them, you can sell or exchange, but a spouse you must keep, no matter whether you have been happy or unhappy in your choice. For here one will declare, You have taken me, now keep me, pleased or displeased.

Thus, too, the Holy Scriptures testify in Judges 14, 1. 2, that Samson went down into a city of the Philistines and there saw a beautiful maiden who pleased him. He then went home again and said to his father and mother, I have seen a virgin whom I love, dear father, get her for me to wife. That was proper.

Again, though children certainly should and must

obey their parents, yet these should be so apt in the exercise of their authority as not by force to oblige or compel them against their will. For there is a proverb that compulsory service is not pleasing to God. For even when children choose each other from desire and love, there will still be a plenty of effort and labor necessary to make marriage happy. It is to be feared, therefore, that where a marriage is not the fruit of inclination and love, the persons being willing, then it will hardly prove to be a happy one and rarely will any good come from it.

Therefore parents should consult their children as to their wish, as Abraham did (Gen. 24, 1 sqq.). For it was with Isaac's consent that his father Abraham did as he wished. Likewise in verse 51, when Abraham's servant comes and woos the bride, they said, Here is Rebecca, take her with you. Then already both were given away to each other. Yet the brother went on and inquired of her whether it was her full wish and will to take Isaac for her husband. To this she said yes (v. 58).

The third thing, then, is this that children or young people, when they wish to get married, do not betroth themselves secretly, without their parents' knowledge, but whatever they do, they should do it with the consent of father and mother; and if their parents are not living, they should get the consent of brothers, relatives or guardians.

If these three things now, which you have heard, have been done, then in God's name let them go forth and get married. And whatever kind of person you may now get, poor or rich, homely or handsome, sick or sound, that is the one whom God has kept and provided for you. Be thankful to God, therefore, and, as we shall hear further on, endeavor to live with your spouse in a godly manner.

This then is the second part, in which we have pointed out how, in order that there may be happiness, one must begin matrimony with God in a godly Christian manner. We shall now consider the third part, viz.,

HOW ONE SHOULD LIVE IN MATRIMONY.

We shall here show, dear friends, how a man and wife, who have married, should live together in wedlock in a godly manner. First, what are the husband's obligations? Secondly, what are the wife's obligations?

When the world hears something concerning matrimony, it says, Yes, it is all right to get married, but how will a man support his wife, for she is a devouring mortgage? These persons I would have learn here how they should support their wives. A man dare not think that he married a wife in order that he, exempt from care, may now loaf and play the gentleman; or that the wife should support him as a young lord; no, on the contrary, the man should support his wife just as a father his child. Yes, you say, wherewith? That you shall now hear. For thus spoke the Lord to Adam after he had listened to the voice of the woman, "In the sweat of thy face shalt thou eat bread, till thou return unto the ground; for out of it wast thou taken: for dust thou art and unto dust shalt thou return" (Gen. 3, 19).

Here you see wherewith you are to support your wife. You are to spit on your hands and take great pains and work hard until the sweat runs down your nose. That is what is required, my dear fellow. Now, to eat bread in the sweat of one's face does not mean

Sermon on Matrimony.

only hard manual labor like that of the farmer, but that every one be diligent in his calling.

If one is a farmer or mechanic, tailor or shoemaker, he should be faithful in his calling. He should not loaf in the saloon and guzzle beer, leaving everything lie at home; he should not spend his evenings with women, when he has no more money for carousals, and sell his poor wife's clothes to the last thread and whatever else she may have. No, that is not the meaning, but in the sweat of thy face, that is, with faithful, diligent labor, you are to support your wife, as Ps. 128, 1. 2. says, "Blessed is every one that feareth the Lord; that walketh in His ways. For thou shalt eat the labor of thine hands: happy shalt thou be, and it shall be well with thee."

This is clear; if you want to be a God-fearing husband and walk in the ways of God, then support yourself by the labor of your hands (2 Thess 3, 12; Eph. 4, 28; Prov. 10, 4). If you do that, God will add His blessing as His Word declares, "Happy shalt thou be and it shall be well with thee." Then, too, will He so bless your labor that you shall be able thereby to support your wife and entire household; and, as we learn from the 34th Psalm, though the rich, who boastingly trust in their riches which they have gathered together, shall suffer want and hunger (for their riches melt away in their hands), yet those who fear the Lord and who, with God and in honor, without any wrong to their neighbor, support themselves by the labor of their hands, shall not want any good thing.

That is, God will so bless their labors, that when they look into the corners of their houses, not one of them shall be found empty. Though both man and wife be poor when they unite, yet God their Father whom they fear and love will (though they may continue in poor circumstances), provide and give them meat and drink, clothing and shelter. We should therefore note well the little word of the Holy Spirit in Ps. 128, 2, "Happy shalt thou be, and it shall be well with thee," and should write it upon the walls of our chambers and rooms and teach it our children.

Furthermore we learn here that the man who does not fear God, nor walk in His ways but in the way of the devil, who does not work and is inclined only to loaf, he shall not prosper but shall be unhappy; that is, God is unmerciful toward him and does not bless his own. On the contrary, he is the devil's martyr and servant, and the devil will see to it also that these persons, when they once have nothing of their own, will allow their hands to cling to that which belongs to their neighbors; afterwards they will be hanged on the towering gallows. Such is the reward of their god, the devil, whom they served.

No, God-fearing men shall not fare thus. When they labor their labor shall be blessed, so that their wants shall be supplied. Though they must take great pains, yet they do not consider that. For they know that it must be so and cannot be otherwise, for here is God's word, "In the sweat of thy face shalt thou eat bread" (Gen. 3, 19).

So, too, a preacher works in the sweat of his face; for working with the head is the severest kind of labor, as when a preacher studies diligently, so that he may, through preaching and the administration of the Sacraments, execute his office. Likewise a prince, nobleman, burgomaster, if they faithfully discharge their duties as rulers; it is all eating one's bread in the sweat of one's face. Happy they! God's blessing shall rest upon them; it shall be well with them, and so shall their position be maintained. This, then, is the first thing, that a man should labor diligently in order to support his wife and children, for work does not kill any one, but by being unoccupied and idle men are ruined in life and limb. For man is born to labor "as the sparks fly upward" (Job. 5, 7).

In the second place, the husband should love his wife as his own body. as St. Paul in Eph. 5, 25. 28 says: Husbands, love your wives as your own bodies; he that loveth his wife loveth himself. Here you see how nicely the apostle teaches how a man should conduct himself toward his wife. He should not look upon her as a foot-mat, for she was not made out of a foot but out of a rib taken from the midst of the man's body, so that he should look upon her not otherwise than upon his own body and flesh; and just as he deals kindly and tenderly with his body (if it is black, he does not reject or disown it; if it is sick, he nurses it and cares for it, and though it does not always serve him alike well, yet he is ready to excuse all), so also should the husband deal with the wife.

And though another woman be prettier, better, more

fluent in conversation, more prudent, wiser and healthier than your wife, yet you should not love her as your own body. No, no; but your wife you should love as your own body. And though she may not always be able to bear herself before you in a like acceptable manner, have patience with her as with your own body, and do as the vinedresser does with a weak vine (for so the Holy Spirit in Ps. 128, 3 calls the wife a vine). When he wants to tie up a vine which, like a wife, is weakly, so that it may bear and produce fruit, he does not use a great iron log-chain, nor a course hempen rope, but a fine pliable band of straw, and with it he ties up the vine.

So, too, women should be governed; not with great knouts, flails, or drawn knives, but with friendly words, friendly gestures and with all gentleness, that, as St. Peter, 1 Epist. 3, 6. 7, says, they do not become timid and frightened and afterwards know not what to do. Women should therefore be ruled with reason and not with unreason, and they should be honored as the weaker vessels and as joint heirs of the grace of life, so that our prayer be not hindered. And that means, as St. Paul writes to the Ephesians (ch. 5, 25), that husbands should love their wives, even as Christ also loved the Church.

We shall now here also tell what the wife should do in the state of matrimony. The wife also has two things to suffer or do. The first, as God says: "I will greatly multiply thy sorrow and thy conception; in sorrow thou shalt bring forth children." That is, if God now gives grace, so that the wife becomes pregnant, two things take place. In the first place, she has great pains and becomes ill, some days she suffers from dizziness, also she has severe attacks of vomititing, neuralgia in her teeth, swelling of the limbs, pain in the bowels; then again she craves coarse unnatural things to eat; if she were well her nature would be shocked at these things. This is one of the things to which the wife in her pregnancy must submit, and endure and bear it.

Afterwards, when the time of her deliverance draws near, then the real suffering and danger just begins. The poor woman, in anguish and labor, even with great danger to her life, must bring forth her child, and many a one also expires in the ordeal (Is. 37, 3;

Sermon on Matrimony.

John 16, 21; Ps. 48, 7). When now the ungodly world sees and hears of such misery and pain, it judges according to reason and feeling and at once declares that it is preferable to remain single, for then one is exempt from all this misery.

But Christian men and Christian women, who have some knowledge of the Word of our Lord God, speak otherwise. And even if they hear of and experience this or that evil in matrimony, what do they do? They first of all see and hear God's word, how God has laid upon them these pains and this affliction. They therefore comfort themselves with His divine and gracious will, saying: I know that such pains, misery and affliction come from no one but the good Lord, who has laid them upon me. Therefore I will willingly endure and suffer them, even if I should die under them.

Therefore women should be encouraged in the labor of childbirth to do their utmost, that is, to exert all their power and strength for the sake of the child.

* * * * *

Thus one should comfort and strengthen a wife in childbirth; not as is done in Popedom, with legends of St. Margaret, or trifle with other foolish foibles of women; but thus one should speak to her: Dear wife, consider that you are a woman and that God is pleased with this work of yours. Comfort yourself with His will and be cheerful and permit Him to have His way with you. If you should die in the act, then go in God's name; happy you, for you die really in the noble work of God and in obedience to His will. Indeed, dear wife, if you were not a woman, you should wish, alone for the sake of this work, to be a woman and that you might suffer and die in such a precious work of God and in obedience to His will. For here is God's word that He has created you thus and has implanted within you such necessity.

Thus Rachel, the wife of the holy patriarch Jacob, died in child labor (Gen. 35, 19). He then buried her by the way as one goes to Bethlehem and not behind the walls in the cemetery, as was done in Popedom, as though women dying in confinement were cursed of God, so that they should not be buried with other Christians in the middle of the cemetery. O, what blindness!

Tell me, now, dear Christian, is not that, as Solomon

says (Prov. 11, 20), finding favor in the sight of God, even in the necessity and pain of childbirth?

St. Paul likewise comforts women in this manner when he says (1 Tim. 2, 14. 15): "Adam was not deceived, but the woman being deceived was in the transgression. Notwithstanding she shall be saved in childbearing, if they continue in faith." This is indeed a great, glorious and comforting word which women should not exchange for all the world's treasures, namely, that their pains and anxiety in childbirth are so highly acceptable and pleasing to God as that they shall be saved therein. What could women hear that is more comforting? God forbid, if nuns in the cloister had the divine assurance that their station is a blessed station, how would they not brag and boast?

Yet we must not understand this as though such salvation were the result simply of bearing children. No; for then would Jewish and Turkish women likewise be saved. But this is said of women who are Christians and who through faith in Jesus Christ have forgiveness of sin, life and salvation.

These are comforted through the assurance that such pains, as fruits of faith, are altogether blessed pains and grief, and are pleasing and a delight to their God and Father. Therefore the beloved Paul says afterwards that the woman shall be saved in childbearing. Yes, how? Thus, that she, that is, the wife or wives, "continue in faith and charity and holiness with sobriety."

This now is the first thing: Wives, when they become pregnant and must bear children, should be patient and should submit, when God lays pain, suffering and trouble upon them, and should deem this all as a blessed and even doubly blessed work of God and pleasing to Him.

In the second place, the wife shall submit her will to that of her husband, as God says (Gen. 3, 16), "Thy desire shall be to thy husband, and he shall rule over thee." That is, the wife shall not exercise her own free will in life as would have been the case, if Eve had not sinned, for then she would have ruled and reigned with Adam, the man as his helpmeet. Now that she has sinned and has deceived the man she has lost this dominion, and must not begin anything nor act without the man. Him she must accompany, and bow herself before him as her lord whom she is to fear, yield to and obey.

This then is the other punishment that the wife must endure because she deceived her husband. And I believe that women would rather and more willingly and patiently endure the former two punishments of pain and trouble connected with childbearing than be subject and obedient to their husbands. So desirous are women by nature, copying after their first mother, Eve, of ruling and exercising authority.

Therefore, too, the beloved apostles frequently speak concerning this in their writings, and especially St. Peter, 1 Epist. 3, 1; and likewise Paul in Eph. 5, 22. 23, where he says, "Wives, submit yourselves unto your own husbands as unto the Lord; for the husband is the head of the wife." Also in Col. 3, 18, the same is said. For that reason, too, the woman was not made from the head that she should rule over the man; on the contrary, she is to be subject and obedient to him. Hence, too, the woman ought to have power on her head, that is, wear a veil, as St. Paul says in 1 Cor. 11, 10, to indicate that she is not free but is in subjection unto the man.

Furthermore, a woman wears a fine delicate veil, spun and made of fine soft linen, and does not wear a coarse, hempen veil or filthy cloth around her head and face. But why? For this reason, because she is expected to address her husband with gentle, loving and friendly words and not approach him, using coarse and filthy terms of abuse, as bad women do who carry a sword in their mouth and afterward receive a beating. Therefore, too, as was said above in Ps. 128, 3, the wife should be of the disposition of a vine, for it allows itself to be bent and twined readily, with a little band of straw, according to the will of the vinedresser. So, too, should wives, in order that we may hear of no cruel flogging and beating, readily permit themselves to be swayed and guided by their husbands by means of words. For so pious, obedient wives are accustomed to say that "unwhipped is best."

This, then, is the second thing that a woman in the state of matrimony has to do; namely, that she should be subject and obedient to her husband and should undertake and do nothing without his will.

The third thing now is, what both man and wife are to do, in case God gives and grants them children, how they are to train them up in the fear of God. For so God commands (Deut. 6, 5. 6. 7, and ch. 11, 19) that when He gives parents children they should teach them to love God with all their heart and with all their soul and with all their might, and that they should diligently teach them God's word; that is, always exercise them with it and remind them of it, so that it may not become rusty and darkened, but continue fresh and clear both in their memory and in deed. For the more one exercises himself with God's word the clearer and newer it becomes, and it is well said, "The longer the better." But when one neglects God's word, it is soon forgotten and loses its efficacy.

Thus God speaks concerning Abraham in Gen, 18, 18. 19, where He says, that "Abraham shall surely become a great and mighty nation, and all the nations of the earth shall be blessed in him. For I know him, that he will command his children and his household after him, and they shall keep the way of the Lord, to do justice and judgment." So St. Paul also teaches in Eph. 6, 4, "Ye fathers, provoke not your children to wrath; but bring them up in the nurture and admonition of the Lord." For a father can well gain salvation with his children, if he brings them up properly; but if he trains them to evil, hell and hell-fire may well be his portion. As people do who accustom their children from youth up to use false measures, weights and wares. And again, they curse and torture them that it is horrible to hear. Woe unto them, at the last day they will have to render a heavy account for their sins. (Matt. 12, 36).

This then is the third thing; parents should bring up their children in the fear of God as God has commanded through Moses. For He has not yet set aside the fourth commandment, to honor father and mother and to obey them.

We have now seen what the duties of husband and wife in the marriage estate are. We shall now speak of the fourth part.

WHETHER HUSBAND AND WIFE MAY AGAIN SEPARATE.

The question now is, may man and wife separate again? Answer: No; for as Christ says in Matt. 19, 6, "What therefore God hath joined together, let no man put asunder." And again in v. 9, "Whosoever

Sermon on Matrimony.

shall put away his wife, except it be for fornication, and shall marry another, committeth adultery." This is also a hard, plain, clear text: this declares that no one, neither for the sake of leprosy, nor foul breath, nor any other weakness, shall leave his wife or the wife the husband; only for the sake of fornication or adultery. These things alone separate man and wife. Yet it must be shown beforehand on sufficient evidence, as justice demands, that fornication and adultery have been committed. Otherwise some might purposely slander their consorts in order to get rid of them. But we say, Prove it first, then let justice have its course.

True; but you may say, How when one has a sickly spouse who is no longer able to perform the marriage duties, may he not take another? By no means, but serve the Lord in the sick consort and wait upon Him. Think that in this way the Lord places an occasion for holy service in your house, by means of which you may gain heaven. Blessed and again blessed are you, if you see in this situation a gift and the grace of God and for His sake minister to your sick spouse.

But you say, It is dangerous to live thus. No; for

if you are in earnest in serving your spouse and know that God so willed it, and if you thank Him and pray Him to keep you, then let Him have the care and surely He will give you grace so that you will not need to bear more than you are able. He is much too faithful (1 Cor. 10, 13) than that He through sickness should rob you of your spouse, and then not, on the other hand, if you only faithfully serve the sick, temper the desires of the flesh.

These, then, are the four parts of which we, on this occasion, wanted to speak. May God give grace that we may duly weigh and consider the great honor of the marriage estate, as we previously heard; that young people may enter upon and begin matrimony in the fear of God; and that afterwards all may live therein in a godly manner, one serving the other in sickness and distress, and not separating; let God alone do this through natural death.

To this help us all, God the Father, God the Son, and God the Holy Ghost. Amen.

MARRIAGE SERMON ON EPH. 5, 22-33.

(Delivered at the Palace of Eilenburg in the year 1536.)

INTRODUCTION.

SINCE we are now celebrating the Easter festival of the joyful resurrection of the Lord Christ and since it is in place also to speak concerning matrimony, both that we may duly honor the estate and praise and thank God, we will upon this occasion combine these two subjects, the resurrection and matrimony, in our discourse. This we will do instead, as was the custom heretofore, of celebrating the spousal mass; for poor service and little favor was thereby rendered unto God because His word was not preached, which, however, is the greatest and most acceptable divine service. We will base our discourse on the following passage from St. Paul's letter to the Ephesians in the 5th chapter:

"Wives, submit yourselves unto your own husbands,

as unto the Lord. For the husband is the head of the wife, even as Christ is the head of the Church: and He is the Savior of the body. Therefore as the Church is subject unto Christ, so let wives be to their own husbands in everything. Husbands, love your wives, even as Christ also loved the Church, and gave Himself for it; that He might sanctify and cleanse it with the washing of water by the word, that He might present it to himself a glorious Church, not having spot or wrinkle, or any such thing; but that it should be holy and without blemish. So ought men to love their wives as their own bodies. He that loveth his wife loveth himself. For no man ever yet hated his own flesh; but nourisheth and cherisheth it, even as the Lord the Church: for we are members of His body, of His flesh, and of His bones. For this cause shall a man leave his father and mother, and shall be joined unto his wife, and they two shall be one flesh. This is a great mystery: but I speak concerning Christ and the Church. Nevertheless let every one of you in particular so love his wife even as himself; and the wife see that she reverence her husband."

MARRIAGE AN EMBLEM OF CHRIST AND HIS CHURCH.

Here St. Paul has combined and woven together into one both the marriage estate and the resurrection, together with the entire kingdom of Christ in Christendom. And he sets before the married, both husband and wife, this one example, that Christ is the head of the Church even as a husband is the head of the wife, and that Christendom is His bride or wife. We then, and all men, who wish to live in Christian marriage and do better than the heathen, are hereby taught to keep in view this image of Christ and His Church, which God has placed before our eyes, in order that in marriage they may keep to it, and may praise and thank God that they are permitted to dwell in these two divine estates, namely, the one, the high spiritual marriage with the Lord Jesus Christ, and the other, the low bodily marriage in the world or in the flesh.

The heathen, it is true, also spoke highly of the marriage estate and held it in honor over against fornication and adultery, but they knew nothing of that high honor which God has bestowed upon the estate, in that He through His own Son has interwoven himself therewith and thereby has united himself to us. They were therefore not able to esteem and honor it so highly as Christians can, who know that Christ Himself is our bridegroom, and that they as Christians and members of His body are His bride and have part in this spiritual marriage relation.

Therefore among us this estate should be esteemed more beautiful and honorable as the example of Christ and the Church is higher, more glorious and precious. And from honor to it we should the more carefully guard ourselves against unchastity and other sins, and maintain the marriage relation pure and holy, as St. Paul admonishes in 1 Thess. 4, 3, "This is the will of God, even your sanctification, that ye should abstain from fornication: that every one of you should know how to possess his vessel in sanctification and honor." "Your sanctification," says he; that is, that you should keep yourselves holy, your body and members in which the soul is contained and dwells as in a vessel, and that you should not do as the heathen who know nothing of God and do not sufficiently honor the marriage estate. Howbeit among those who call themselves Christians there are also many who in these things live as do the swine and irrational brutes. You, however, should honor your body and this bodily life in the estate of matrimony and its external connections, and should look upon it as ordained of God according to the high and glorious image of Christ and the Church, through which it is honored and sanctified; to the end that you may prosper accordingly and show yourselves thankful for being permitted to enjoy and participate in its blessings.

For it is bestowing upon the estate of matrimony not a little honor and glory, that God should represent and portray it as an image and illustration of the high and unspeakable grace and love which He manifests and graciously bestows in Christ, even as the most certain and delightful token of the highest and most friendly union between himself and the Church with all her members; than which we cannot conceive of a union more close. And He has hereby sufficiently indicated that this estate is a divine one and pleasing to Him, because He has chosen to use it for so holy an example or illustration of the spiritual marriage, out of which His heart and will shine upon us and in which we should daily see ourselves reflected; and especially should those who are married comfort themselves with one another in their estate, as St. Paul here admonishes.

Therefore St. Paul here depicts these things concerning Christian marriage, with many beautiful and glorious words, how Christ loved the Church and prepared her as a pure beautiful bride, etc. He draws in also (as I have said) His resurrection through which these things have been accomplished. For thus says He to His disciples in the Gospel, John 20, 21 (which is read upon this day), "As the Father hath sent me, so send I you — whosesoever sins ye remit, they are remitted unto them," etc. Here He himself institutes this marriage as the fruit and result of His resurrection. For this sending forth of the apostles is nothing else than what we in German call, Sending out suitors, who shall woo the bride and conduct her to the bridegroom. So (says St. Paul here), has Christ chosen Himself a bride, even the Christian communion or Church, and has prepared the same for Himself through the Word and baptism with water. This has been accomplished through the apostles who were sent out by Him and whose office was instituted that we might be called and brought to Christ and through it also be sanctified and purified, so that we might be betrothed and united with Him.

Thus St. Paul glories in himself as such a messenger or suitor, sent out by Christ, when he says in 2 Cor. 11, 2, "For I am jealous over you with godly jealousy: for I have espoused you to one husband, that I may present you as a chaste virgin to Christ." He hereby indicates that the apostolic office is nothing other than the office of a suitor or bridesman who daily prepares and presents to Christ Jesus His bride. So also did the servant of Abraham, who procured a bride for his son Isaac, Gen. 24. This office Christ here first laid upon His apostles as though He had said unto them, I send you forth to woo and get for me my bride, yet so that she shall first be prepared, that is, washed clean from sin, in order that she may be pure and holy.

CHRIST WOOING HIS BRIDE.

These things are being accomplished daily in the Christian Church by means of the office of the ministry which declares, first, as St. Paul here states, that Christ gave Himself for the Church, etc. This was done when He suffered and died upon the cross and rose again the third day. For thereby He gained for us mercy and the forgiveness of sins. But if nothing more had been done, we would not have been rescued. For although He had won for us the treasure and had finished all things, yet we could not have procured it. How come we now to possess that sanctification which He has accomplished for us? For He has ascended up into heaven and has left us here beneath.

Thus it is done, says He; it must be applied to us through the word and baptism which the apostles were commanded to bring and apply to us, namely, that through these they should convey to us the forgiveness of sins in His name. Thus He indeed continues above at the right hand of the Father, yet through His apostles and ministers of the Gospel He brings us to Himself, just as He through St. Paul gathered to Himself the congregation at Corinth, in Galatia, at Ephesus and many others. Accordingly, then, the sanctification which He has procured for us is applied through the preaching of the Gospel and through baptism. And wherever this word is preached and heard there is heard the wooing of the Bridegroom's messengers. And whoever receives this word and believes it and is baptized, he is thereby fitted, cleansed, washed and made holy, according to Christ's will, and conducted to Him as His bride. By means of this command of Christ, that all who believe the apostles' preaching concerning the forgiveness of sins shall have their sins remitted and shall be clean, the whole world, and at last we also, have been brought together and incorporated with His bride, the Church. For although we do not hear the apostles themselves, yet we hear the same word and through it receive the same grace and sanctification.

For furthermore, the word and its effect or power are not of the apostles, but they are Christ's own word and work. Thus, too, the apostle declares here: He himself, not the apostles, nor other messengers or preachers, has cleansed and sanctified the Church. For they are far too weak that they should wash and cleanse me; indeed they need this washing and cleansing themselves as much as I or any one else. But we become pure and holy thereby, declares he, that Christ has given Himself for us and that this is now offered and appropriated to us through the preaching of the word.

Therefore it does not matter to me through whom, whether the person be holy or not, or when or where the Lord grants me to hear these things and to be baptized, but it depends solely upon this, that it be the Lord Christ's word and baptism. When I hear that word I hear Christ's servants who for His sake have come to bring me to Him as His bride.

THE GREATNESS OF THE GIFT.

This then, as St. Paul declares, is the great and unspeakable grace and gift which God has granted unto Christians, though before the world there is no glory here. For consider thou how great must be the honor and glory, that Christ, the Son of God, has so deeply humbled Himself and has assumed such friendly relations toward us, as not simply to be called our Lord, Father, brother or friend and the like, but has selected that name which represents the greatest love and the most intimate friendship upon earth, even that He wishes to be called and be our bridegroom, and so, as we say of man and wife, be one body with us; or, as the Scriptures say, of one flesh and bone. This cannot be said of any other relation or friendship. Thus has He shown Himself toward us in the most loving and friendly manner and has offered and assured to us His highest love, to the end that we should be called His beloved bride and that we might with all confidence claim and glory in Him as our beloved spouse.

Therefore St. Paul speaks of matrimony in such a distinguished manner and so magnifies it as though he could not sufficiently describe it in words, and hence stops short by saying, This is a great mystery. He would thereby say, That which God wishes to express in the estate of matrimony is an exceedingly great, glorious and unspeakable thing. But I speak, says he, concerning Christ and the Church, that is, concerning the spiritual marriage. This, however, is a mystery, that is, a hidden secret thing which cannot be known through reason or from the appearance of things, but alone by the spirit through faith and according to the word. For since the word and baptism, or the washing with water, appears to be such simple and insignificant means, no one can see nor at the present feel what a queen I have become through them, if I believe in Christ. In short, both the marriage and the bride and the bridegroom himself, as also all the treasures and blessings therein received, are secret and hidden to us. That so great and glorious a thing should be accomplished herein is too high for human reason and sense, and it can simply not be known nor comprehended except alone through the two outward elements of word and water.

For I indeed hear the declaration how God through Christ bestows upon me as His bride the gifts of grace and makes me partaker of all His heavenly and eternal treasures. I see very well, too, that thou art baptized unto these things with water. But when I look upon thee I see nothing of the kind. For I see nothing else than that thou livest in the body, dost eat and drink, dost labor and do all things in this external life, just like another man, and that in these things a heathen may be like thee. But the glory and adornment which has become thine through Christ I cannot see, nor canst thou thyself, except in so far as

Marriage Sermon on Ephesians 5, 22-33.

thou perceivest it by faith; and if we could see and feel what we have in these things, I take it that we would then already be in heaven.

For what greater joy and blessedness could a man desire than that he should be able to believe firmly and without doubt and to boast with his whole heart: Christ is one body with me and as a bridegroom with the bride, so does He share with me all that He is and has. Here everything, body, goods, honor, is common possession as of one; everything is undivided. All other friends and estates are separated and divided: children from their parents, brothers and sisters from the same house and home. But this estate binds and retains all things together so that on its account a man will leave father and mother and all things else, and, if conjugal love is of the right kind, one will even hazard his life for the other.

So, says St. Paul, has Christ dealt with His Church. He loved her and gave Himself for her in order that we might be one body with Him and have all things in Him, and that we might own Him and His heavenly glory and comfort ourselves therewith as with our own. O, it is a great and glorious thing — who can sufficiently declare it and comprehend and consider it? — that a poor worm, conceived and born in sin, should attain to such glory as to be called the bride of the majesty of heaven, that is, of the Son of God, and that He should unite Himself with us so that all that He is and has is ours, and again that we together with what pertains to us are His. But what is He? And what are we? He is the beautiful Bridegroom, altogether pure and without any blemish, the Lord of all creatures, the everlasting righteousness, everlasting strength and everlasting life. In short, He is the pure, everlasting and incomprehensible good which no heart can sufficiently comprehend nor weigh, and upon which both men and angels throughout eternity will delight to look. We, on the contrary, are poor miserable creatures, full of sin and uncleanness from the sole of our foot to the crown of our head, corrupted through and through, subject to the devil, and under the wrath of God condemned to death and damnation.

Therefore, it must be unspeakable grace, yea the very fire and ardency of love, which moves Him to

Marriage Sermon on Ephesians 5, 22-33.

humble Himself so deeply and willingly give Himself to us, and to go to such great costs in order to bring us to Himself. He does not hesitate to shed His precious blood and suffer the most shameful death in order that we may be called His bride and possess His treasures, namely, everlasting righteousness, freedom, blessedness and life, instead of the sin, death, and devil's power in which we lay. He devotes to us all His purity that He may free us from sin; all His honor that He may cover and take away our shame; His body and life that he may rescue us from death; all His heavenly treasures and power that He may free us from this destitute and miserable existence and bring us to His own glory. So also the sin and weakness which still adhere to us shall not hurt us, the devil shall not accuse us, the law shall not condemn, death shall not destroy, etc. For He stands before us and says, Do not molest My bride; if anything be lacking in her, I will supply it. If she is not sufficiently beautiful and pure, I can make her pure and beautiful. If thou art not pleased with her, it is of no consequence; it is enough that I am pleased. For I have chosen and cleansed her for myself and

I still cleanse her daily through the word and baptism. And through sin, death and other weaknesses still cling to her, I, on the contrary, have righteousness, life and all eternal treasures, and with these I adorn her that she should accept them as her own.

Behold, these are the high, heavenly treasures and goods that are eulogized here, and, as St. Paul declares, they indeed are and continue a mystery, a secret hidden boon which the world neither sees nor knows, and so great, too, as that Christians who embrace it by faith can neither reach nor comprehend it. And he whose heart could fully grasp it could not for joy continue long upon the earth. But here in our flesh and blood is that miserable wretchedness which does not permit us to enter into the glorious thoughts, and therefore we canot rightly consider these things, nor estimate them at their actual greatness. Our heart is far too narrow and weak and the glory of this spiritual marriage far too great that we should be able to grasp it; so also Christ the bridegroom and the purity and glory which are His own are far beyond us, and the love which He herein manifests toward us is inconceivable.

Yet thence we are also comforted with the assurance that He bears our daily weaknesses, and excuses us, if only we hold fast to Him. For He must still daily and constantly cleanse us, and when blemishes and spots appear He covers them over with His righteousness and purity in order that we may still continue in honor and may cheerfully call Him our bridegroom, saying, However things may be about me, I will remain with my beloved bridegroom. If any one finds fault with me, let him complain to Him, for it is His will and He tells me so, that if I believe in Him I will continue to be His bride. To this has He brought me through the word and baptism which He has granted me to receive through beloved ministers of the Gospel.

This is what Christians do and ought to do, namely, thank, honor and praise God that he has shown Himself so merciful towards us and has imparted Himself to us. For, as has been sufficiently stated, in this spiritual marriage there is included all that He has and can give, and there has been established a common ownership of possessions between us and Him, so that all His righteousness becomes ours, and all our sins and weaknesses become His. Of this He has given ample proof and to us He still gives proof thereof. For in Christ He has taken upon Himself and has born the sin of the whole world and hence also your sin and mine; even as St. Paul says, 2 Cor. 5, 21, "He hath made Him to be sin for us, who knew no sin; that we might be made the righteousness of God in Him;" and in addition He has sent forth His messengers that they through the Word and baptism might convey these things unto us.

Let us therefore as Christians who should be aware of their treasure and glory, also learn to boast of this marriage, to comfort ourselves therewith and rejoice in it, for through the grace of God we have attained unto the high honor of being the bride of Christ His Son. Of this I am convinced, for I have the word and baptism, and I have begun to believe; and I am sure that, if I continue therein, God has accepted me and adorned me with His ornaments, taking away every spot and blemish and cleansing me more and more. If now thou art His bride, then hast thou the treasure in thine hand and art mistress in the house, sitting in the midst of His heavenly treasures, as St. Paul says in Eph. 1, 4, that neither sin, nor death, nor devil shall henceforth have any power or claim upon thee.

Behold, such is the exalted discourse and precious example that St. Paul teaches us to make use of when we are treating of marriage or the estate of matrimony; to the end that those who are about to enter into this estate, or are already therein, may be instructed and reminded of these things, and that when they contemplate their estate they may recall these words, and hold up before their own eyes this image or example of spiritual marriage. For we do well to call that a great, glorious marriage institution or wedding and a precious royal adornment by means of which we have been made partakers, not of bodily goods, but of salvation from sin and death and of all divine treasures. Compared with these, bodily adornment and worldly treasures are very small, even if thou shouldst receive tuns of gold, yea all the treasures of kings and emperors. For all these things a man can measure with his eye and compass them. Likewise the question as to what the bride and groom are in bodily respects is not so important, for they are poor, mortal, human beings. Yet these outward and visible matters of a wedding and of natural marriage should lead us to look and reflect on the spiritual whose glory and graces no eye can measure. And on the other hand, we should see reflected in the spiritual union between Christ and the Church, how man and wife should live together in the marriage estate.

THE HOLY DUTIES OF MAN AND WIFE.

Paul has a text therefore also for those who are married, for he says, "As the Church is subject unto Christ, so let the wives be to their own husbands in everything." And again he says, "Husbands, love your wives, even as Christ loved the Church, and gave himself for it." He thereby declares that man and wife should consider how the two, Christ and His Church, deport themselves towards one another, and should diligently follow this example, for this is the highest and most perfect pattern and a true and faithful mirror. For here the state is this that Christ loves the Church, even so as to have given Himself for it.

To this love we shall by no means attain, for, as

has been said, it is far too high and great. And as natural marriage is a little thing, so also is the love thereof compared with that of the spiritual feeble. It must suffice therefore to follow the example and to endeavor to reach the measure of the spiritual marriage, to the end that every one in the marriage estate be minded to manifest and exercise love toward his spouse. And though he may discover defects and infirmities in her, he should excuse these and should act with reason and say, What shall I do? This I should do: she is my bride and here I should conceal, purify, adorn and improve as much as I can, and I should show the little love in this little marriage even as Christ exhibits high, unspeakable love towards His bride of which I also am a member.

Again, says he, the wife should be subject and obedient to her husband, even as the Church is subject unto Christ. Here he does not command the bride or wife to love the husband, but that she should honor him and be subject unto him; yet this cannot be done without love. For if I do not love a person, I will not wish him honor and wellbeing, nor will I be much inclined to obey and serve him. Wherefore if this honor and submission are to be of the right kind, they must spring from love, that the wife may know and believe that the husband is higher and greater than she. For as head and master in the house, government and authority belong to the husband, as St. Paul elsewhere says, that "he is the image and glory of God" (1 Cor. 11, 7). Likewise in 1 Cor. 11, 9, "Neither was the man created for the woman; but the woman for the man," etc. Therefore the distinction is made that the husband should indeed love the wife, but should not be subject unto her. The wife, on the other hand, should honor and fear the husband with all modesty and respect.

For thus the Church seeks to honor her Bridegroom who is Christ, her Lord and head, and is obedient and subject to Him in all things. That is, she continues in the pure faith, lives according to His command and does whatever she knows to be His will; unless it be that the devil should come in and corrupt the bride. For so St. Paul is concerned for his church, saying in 2 Cor. 11, 2, "I have espoused you to one husband, that I may present you as a chaste virgin to Christ," but something troubles me and I am concerned for you, yea, I am envious and jealous of you (yet with godly jealousy, not from hatred or anger), lest you should be won for another. For I fear nothing so much as that the devil may beguile you and rend you from Christ. So it befell Eve in Paradise; she was a beautiful bride, adorned with all manner of graces, both external and with spiritual and divine favors, and was obedient and subject to God. But the devil beguiled her and effected her fall, so that she fell away from God and, following the adulterer, she has brought us, together with herself, to the harm which we suffer.

So, says he, I am concerned for you who have been brought to Christ and have become His bride. For the danger is great, since the devil without let is besetting the Church, while we on our part are weak; and ye need therefore to take heed with all diligence, lest through the cunning and craft of the devil ye be turned from the word and obedience of Jesus Christ, who loved you and gave himself for you. We see how now and all along many Christians have been deceived through sects and schisms, and how under the Pope the whole world has with his sanction been filled with spiritual fornication and adultery and the bride of Christ corrupted, so that it was impossible to recognize her until Christ now again has begun to cleanse her with His word. Behold, that is what he means when he says that the Church is to be obedient and subject to Christ in all things; she is to keep herself only to Him and be guided solely by His word, not following those who would teach and direct her otherwise.

In like manner also the wife in the estate of matrimony should not only love her husband, but also be obedient and subject to him. She should be teachable and cheerfully submit to his rule and, showing due homage, should keep herself unto him alone and be governed by his will. And these things she should do, not simply considering that he has authority over her, but she should see in him the true and great head, Christ himself, and should for His sake honor him and do those things which please him.

Likewise the husband, on the other hand, should heartily love his wife for the sake of that great love which he sees in Christ who gave himself for us; and he should also think, Neither I nor any one else has done as Christ has; therefore I will make every endeavor, after this example, to deport myself in love toward my wife as toward my own flesh, so that I may nourish, cherish and wait upon her and not be bitter against her nor whimsical, but bear with her in reason and patience, if she have any fault or weakness, or else seek her improvement through friendly admonition and correction. Such a marriage would no longer be a worldly and human, or a merely natural marriage, but a Christian and divine one, of which the heathen know nothing, for they do not see the great adornment and honor of marriage, inasmuch as it is the image of the high, spiritual marriage of Christ. Therefore, as I have said, it becomes us Christians to esteem and honor this estate very highly, since we know and are aware of the great honor and glory attached to it. Be not surprised, though thou seest the world lying as it does in fornication and adultery, yea even the false, senseless saints, belittling this estate. We, however, should justly esteem it as the very greatest estate, for no other estate has been elevated by God to such high honor. And we should know that those, (especially those who wish to be known as Christians), who despise it, not only defame it before the world, but also cast dishonor and disgrace upon the high and holy marriage of Christ and the Church; and thereby they unmistakably show that they think but little of the latter, since they despise the lesser and external marriage estate.

Let this suffice at this time concerning this text of St. Paul in which he admonishes Christians to consider the matter and not, as the world and the natural heart do, simply look at this estate with reference to external things, but that they should look farther and higher and see in it the beautiful comforting image of Christ and the Church, and should accordingly esteem and honor the marriage estate; and this they should do not simply because God has so ordained and commanded, but also in honor of the great spiritual marriage, in order that one may perceive that they also desire to be found in this. For we should not permit such glory and comfort to be taken from before our eyes and out of our heart and cast into the hedge, as the monks and nuns have done, who have arrogated these things unto themselves and have despised and belittled the marriage estate, by representing their false and self-invented priesthood as being alone the bride of Christ; notwithstanding that Paul contrariwise and purposely magnifies the marriage estate and presents to the married the great example of Christ's marriage to the Church. Amen.

LUTHERAN MARRIAGE SERVICE.

DEARLY BELOVED, forasmuch as marriage was instituted by God himself, and is honorable in all, it becomes those who would enter into this estate duly to weigh what the Scripture saith concerning it. Let us therefore, for the glory of God, and for the instruction, admonition and comfort of these persons here present, hear some portions of Scripture thereto pertaining.

In the second chapter of Genesis we read: "The Lord God said, It is not good that the man should be alone; I will make a helpmeet for him. Therefore shall a man leave his father and mother, and shall cleave unto his wife; and they shall be one flesh."

Hear also the Lord's command concerning this estate. St. Paul writes, "Husbands, love your wives, even as Christ also loved the Church, and gave himself for it. So ought men to love their wives as their own bodies; he that loveth his wife loveth himself. For no man ever yet hated his own flesh; but nourisheth and cherisheth it, even as the Lord the Church. Wives, submit yourselves unto your husbands, as unto the Lord. For the husband is the head of the wife, even as Christ is the head of the Church. Therefore as the Church is subject unto Christ, so let the wives be to their own husbands in everything."

But you should also remember, that by reason of our manifold sins, God has appointed that those who enter into this estate should also bear the cross. You cannot therefore expect always to enjoy prosperity; days of adversity will also come; but if you fear God and keep His commandments, He will not forsake you. He will strengthen and keep you in every time of need, and comfort you in all your sorrows.

As you have now been shown what the word of God teaches concerning marriage, I exhort you diligently to consider the same, and to strive to conform your lives thereto.

As no impediments have been shown, why you may not be lawfully joined together in matrimony; I ask you in the presence of God, and of these witnesses:

N. Do you take this woman to your wedded wife,

to live together after God's ordinance in the holy estate of matrimony? Will you love her, comfort her, honor and keep her, as a faithful Christian husband is bound to do, in health and in sickness, in prosperity and in adversity; and forsaking all others, keep you only unto her, so long as you both shall live?

Answer, Yes.

N. Do you take this man to your wedded husband, to live together after God's ordinance in the holy estate of matrimony; will you love him, obey him, honor and keep him, as a faithful Christian wife is bound to do, in health and in sickness, in prosperity and adversity; and forsaking all others, keep you only unto him, so long as you both shall live?

Answer, Yes.

[If a ring is to be used the minister then says:]

You will now according to ancient usage, witness your troth by the use of the ring.

The ring is an emblem of eternity. Its precious material is a type of the bright and pure affection which should mark the relations of holy wedlock. It is worn as a band of ornament and grace. And with this ring you do each other wed.

(*Here handing it to the man to be placed by him upon the finger of the woman, the minister continues*:)

Thus enduring, pure and excellent be the bonds of that union of love, to which you mutually testify!

Join your right hands.

What God hath joined together, let no man put asunder.

Forasmuch as these two, N. and N., have consented together in holy wedlock, and have witnessed the same before God and these witnesses, I pronounce them man and wife, in the name of the Father, and of the Son, and of the Holy Ghost. Amen.

Let us pray:

Almighty and most Merciful God, who didst institute the holy estate of matrimony, and in Thy good providence dost permit these Thy servants to enter into the same; we render Thee most hearty thanks for this Thy goodness; and we beseech Thee to grant them Thy grace, that they may lead a holy Christian and godly life, in accordance with the teachings of Thy holy Word. Let Thy heavenly blessing abide upon them, that they may be defended against all temptation to sin, and be kept from all danger and harm. Remove from them all discord and contention; strengthen them to constant fidelity and sincere affection toward each other; and preserve them with all Thy true followers, in steadfastness of faith, in the knowledge of Thy dear Son, and in patience under trials to the end of their lives; for the sake of our Savior Jesus Christ, who liveth and reigneth with Thee, in the unity of the Holy Spirit, ever one God. Amen.

Our Father, who art in heaven, etc.

The Lord bless thee and keep thee. The Lord make His face shine upon thee and be gracious unto thee; the Lord lift up His countenance upon thee and give thee peace. Amen.

WEDDING HYMN.

O Jesus Christ, how bright and fair
The state of holy marriage, where
Thy blessing rich is given!
With gracious gifts Thou dost bestow,
What streams of bounty ever flow
Down from Thy holy heaven.
    When they
        Obey
    Thee, Lord, ever,
        Leave Thee never,
    Who, troth plighted,
    In one life have been united.

When man and wife are mated well,
In harmony together dwell
    In chaste and faithful union,
Then grows their fortune with their love,
And angel visitants above
    Rejoice at such communion;
        No storm,

      No worm
    Can destroy that,
      Can e'er gnaw that,
Which God giveth
To the pair that in Him liveth.

Be of good cheer, it was not we
Who first this order did decree;
  It was a higher Father,
Who loved and loveth us for aye,
And from whose lips, when grieved, each day,
  We friendly counsel gather;
    Good end
      He'll send
    To our doing
      And pursuing,
    Wisely guiding
All our planning and providing.

A time will come, it cannot fail,
When we 'neath trials sore shall quail,
  And tears be freely flowing;
To him who bears it patiently,

Wedding Hymn.

By God's grace shall his sorrow be
  Turned into joy o'erflowing.
    Waive care,
        Wait, bear;
    He is near thee,
        Who can cheer thee,
    For thy sadness
    He will give thee oil of gladness.

Come hither, then, my King, so blessed!
In trials guide, in pain give rest,
  In anxious times relieving!
To Thee we shall ascribe the praise,
Our hearts and voices we shall raise
  In our loud song, thanks giving,
    Till we
        With Thee
    Shall be dwelling,
        And there telling
    Thy praise ever,
    Nevermore from Thee to sever.

Composer, PAUL GERHARDT.
Translator, J. KELLY.

CPSIA information can be obtained at www.ICGtesting.com
Printed in the USA
LVOW041330270112

265827LV00001B/32/A

9 781585 090143